Teens, Depression, and the Blues

Teens, Depression, and the Blues

A Hot Issue

Kathleen Winkler

Enslow Publishers, Inc.

40 Industrial Road   PO Box 38
Box 398   Aldershot
Berkeley Heights, NJ 07922   Hants GU12 6BP
USA   UK
http://www.enslow.com

Library of Congress Cataloging-in-Publication Data

Winkler, Kathleen.
    Teens, depression, and the blues : a hot issue / Kathleen
Winkler.
        p.   cm. — (Hot issues)
    Includes bibliographical references and index.
    Summary: Discusses the causes, symptoms, and sometimes
deadly effects of depression and provides information on where
help is available for those suffering from this illness.
    ISBN 0-7660-1369-3
    1. Depression in adolescence Juvenile literature. 2. Teenagers—
Mental health Juvenile literature. [1. Depression, Mental.] I. Title.
II. Series.
RJ506.D4W56   2000
616.85'27'00835—dc21   99-36659
                                        CIP

Printed in the United States of America

10 9 8 7 6 5 4 3 2 1

To Our Readers:
All Internet addresses in this book were active and appropriate when we
went to press. Any comments or suggestions can be sent by e-mail to
Comments@enslow.com or to the address on the back cover.

Illustration Credits: AP/Wide World Photos, pp. 18, 22, 38, 46, 52;
© Corel Corporation p. 41; Skjold Photos, pp. 3, 10, 33.

Cover Illustration: Skjold Photos

Contents

Chapter 1

Two Stories of Depression

Most people who meet Kelly—with her many friends and straight-*A* grades—would think of her as someone with no problems.

They would be wrong.

Kelly is just pulling out of a depression that caused her to hate herself and her life. It stole the sunshine from her days and filled them with a gray fog until she could hardly get out of bed each morning.

Kelly's story proves an important point: One cannot always tell what is going on inside someone by what is seen on the outside.

"I was having so many problems," Kelly says, looking back two years to her freshman year of high school. "My parents are divorced. It happened when I was six and I've been hurting ever since."[1]

There have been so many things that still cause her pain: Her father's remarriage to a woman only ten years older than Kelly, her mother's remarriage, and problems getting along with both stepparents. Kelly also had to move back and forth between both houses. She began having trouble with her father's new wife and rarely saw her father or her two new half-sisters. Even worse, her parents said that problems they were having were all her fault for not cooperating. The last straw was when the boyfriend Kelly cared about dumped her. Kelly describes how all this affected her:

> I started not being able to sleep because so many things were going through my mind. I had headaches I'd never had before. I cried all the time. I started not caring about how I looked. I wouldn't wash my hair or do my makeup; I'd go to school in old sweatpants and T-shirts. I stopped caring about my life, about what was going on around me. I felt like no one cared about me, that I was all alone.[2]

Her friends did not understand what was happening to her. Sometimes they would find her crying, and she could not even tell them why. "I couldn't control it, I couldn't stop it," she says.[3]

Kelly started trying to hide what was happening to her:

> I got really good at acting like everything was fine in my family life, like I didn't have any problems. I told my best friends what was really going on and they knew it was hard, but even they didn't really know how much I was going through. I'd cry when I was by myself. Sometimes I'd be real quiet when I was with them and when they asked what was wrong, I'd just say "nothing," because even I didn't know how bad it really was. Feeling sad starts to feel normal after a while.[4]

Kelly's grades dropped from straight A's to D's and F's. Her family just shrugged it off and stopped expecting anything more. She did not even want to try.

Kelly tried alcohol to dull the pain, but it did not work. "It made my life worse, made me even more depressed," she says. "I wasn't solving a problem, I was just causing another one."[5]

Thoughts of ending her life kept pushing into Kelly's mind. "I seriously considered suicide," she says. "Once I tried to cut my wrists—I can't swallow pills—but I got too scared and didn't complete it. I thought about my younger brother and my two little sisters and that stopped me."[6]

All through the bleak, black days, Kelly's parents did not seem to know how bad she was feeling. "I didn't want to be called depressed," she says. "I just told myself that I was going through some hard times. But it was getting worse."[7]

At first, Kelly did not want to get help. She felt people would look down on her if she went to see a professional. But then, Kelly's father asked her to go to a psychologist to see if she and her stepmother could get along a little better. At first she said no, but then she decided to give it a try.

The psychologist determined that Kelly was depressed. He gave her some tools to use in dealing with the family problems that were part of her depression. She only went to the psychologist for a few months, but it made a big difference in her life.

"The counselor [psychologist] told me that what my parents said—if they got divorced again from their new spouses it would be my fault—wasn't true," she says,

> He made me see that my family had problems and was really dysfunctional. Knowing that helped a lot. He made me feel better about myself, boosted my self-esteem. He was on my side. He helped me see that other kids have divorced parents they don't get along with too.

*T*eens who stop going out with friends and start spending a lot of time alone may be showing signs of depression.

You feel a lot better when you know that you're not the only one.[8]

Gradually, Kelly says, getting to the bottom of her feelings about her family started making her feel a little better. "You do learn some things from your problems, and I started acting on what I was learning," she says.[9]

Kelly started going out with her friends more instead of saying no. She began to have fun and laugh again. "When you have some things that make you happy, your whole life gets better," she says.[10]

But it did not happen in a flash. "I didn't wake up one day and think 'Hey, I'm going to be happy all the time from now on,'" she says. "In fact, I'm still working on it."[11]

Kelly's grades are back to all *A*'s again, and she is thinking about college. "I have plans for my future now and they're all positive. Before I didn't care if I lived to the next day. Now I'm excited about my future."[12]

Things do not go as well for all depressed kids as they did for Kelly, however. Annie is an example— her depression has not gone away.

Annie's depression did not seem to be caused by any single life event. But during the summer before her junior year in high school she gradually started feeling kind of down. "I wasn't my normal self," she says. "I was crying a lot off and on, and feeling kind of irritable. Then, when the school year started, it really came on."[13]

It was the crabbiness that really got her into trouble. She and a friend had a disagreement at school. "I tried to walk away and she pushed me, so

I punched her," Annie says. "That got me suspended."[14]

When she got home from school her mother had found a razor blade Annie had hidden in her closet. Between that and the suspension, Annie's mom decided she needed help and took her to a hospital with a mental-health unit. "At first I was upset about going, but then I decided to give it a try," Annie says.[15]

Annie was in the hospital for five days. Most of the time she spent in group therapy with other kids and a mental-health professional. She also met with a psychiatrist who put her on medication for her depression. Although she did not like being in the hospital while she was there, she now realizes it was helpful. "It was good to talk about things and to get them off my chest," she says. "The medicine didn't do much at first, but after a couple of weeks it started to help."[16]

When she left the hospital, Annie went to a psychologist for a while, but she moved away. Now Annie is looking for another psychologist and hopes to get back into therapy soon. "I know the medication can't do it all," she says. "I have to work at it, too. I'm not over it yet; I still have times when I just break down and have to take time out. It's really up and down."[17]

Annie's mother has been treated for both depression and bulimia (an eating disorder in which the person eats a lot and then throws up) and understands what her daughter is going through. Annie's grandmother was also depressed.

Annie still is not certain what set off her depression. "I have lots of friends and I used to be in a lot of stuff at school—especially track. Now I'm not in anything," she says. "My friends are really there for me, but sometimes they say, 'How can you be feeling this way if you don't know what's causing it?'"[18]

Annie says she knows she would never kill herself, but she has used scissors to cut her arms. "It takes out a lot of anger," she says. "A lot of my depression still comes out as anger. I don't even know what I'm mad at—little things trigger me."[19] Annie's impulse to hurt herself is a strong sign that her depression is still dangerous.

Looking toward the future is hard. "I used to know what I wanted, but now I can't see past today," she says.[20]

Two young women with clinical depression: One with a fairly mild condition, which she was able to overcome with a little help, and one with a deep depression she is not over yet. Their struggles are not unusual. Lots of teenagers, about a million and half each year, according to the National Institute of Mental Health, become depressed.[21] Eighty percent do not realize what is wrong and do not get any help.[22]

In order to understand depression, it is important to look at what it is like, what causes it, and how it is treated. One should also learn how to know when he or she is depressed, how to tell if a friend is, and what to do to get help.

Chapter 2

What Is This Thing Called Depression?

What is life: A bowl of cherries? A beach? A ride at Disneyland?

Maybe, for some teenagers. But for most people, life is downs as well as ups. Sometimes you make the basketball team, sometimes you are on the cut list. Sometimes your parents are warm and seem to care about you; sometimes they are so wrapped up in their own problems they do not see yours. Pets or loved ones can get sick and die.

Any of those things could cause somebody to be sad. That is perfectly normal—sad events make sad feelings. Add the stew of hormones in a teenage body, and those feelings can become even harder to manage.

But when do those sad feelings cross the line and become depression? *Depression* is a medical term. It is defined in *Mosby's Medical and Nursing Dictionary* as "An abnormal emotional state characterized by exaggerated feelings of sadness, melancholy, dejection, worthlessness, emptiness and hopelessness that are out of proportion to reality."[1] In simple terms, it means feeling really bad about oneself and one's life.

The difference between sad feelings and real depression can be hard to figure out. "Depression is different from an event, like getting a poor grade on a test or having a fight with a friend," says Dr. Kathleen Longeway, a psychologist who works with young people. "Then you know why you're upset and it usually passes in a few days. If you don't know why you're upset, if you don't know what to do about what is upsetting you, if you are always crabby and have trouble concentrating, you may be in a depression."[2]

There are different types of depression. Most mental-health professionals talk about two main kinds—dysthymic disorder and major depression.

Dysthymic Disorder

Also called chronic depression, dysthymic disorder is a kind of general depression, not linked with any one event, that just seems to go on forever. "Some people describe it as being a little more crabby, a little more gloomy than usual," says Dr. Longeway. "It comes on gradually."[3] It may be caused by brain chemicals, or it could have a genetic link. To be diagnosed as chronic depression, the symptoms have to last for a year (two years in adults) and happen more days than not. There cannot be more than two months in that year without symptoms. Along with the gloomy mood may come not eating or eating too much, not sleeping or sleeping too much, low energy and self-esteem, poor concentration, and feelings of hopelessness. Some people think of it as less serious than other kinds of depression, but that is not really true. Dysthymic disorder is only about half as common as major depression, but it lasts longer. Chronic depression can make it hard for a person to live normally and can be hard to treat. Also, people who have it are at higher risk of getting major depression later.[4] In fact, 10 percent of people who have it will have a major depression within a year.[5]

Major Depression

This disorder has been described as a whole-body illness because it affects much more than just the mind. Major depression can come on slowly or suddenly. Many different things can cause it, such as a chemical imbalance in the brain or a family genetic pattern. Some feelings and behavior that raise a red warning flag are:

- ➤ Feelings of extreme sadness, sometimes without knowing what is causing them.

- ➤ Frequent crying spells.

- ➤ Feelings of irritability—getting mad over nothing.

- ➤ Loss of interest in activities the person used to enjoy.

- ➤ Withdrawal from family and friends.

- ➤ Changes in appetite and either gaining or losing weight.

- ➤ Changes in sleep patterns: Sleeping too much, too little, or at the wrong time of day.

- ➤ Feeling guilty about things the person did not cause, constant self-criticism.

- ➤ Feeling worthless or ugly, being overly sensitive to any kind of criticism.

➤ Needing to be told over and over that family and friends care.

➤ Feeling hopeless, as though there were no way to solve problems.

➤ Not being able to think well.

➤ Trouble making decisions.

➤ Trouble remembering things.

➤ Tiredness, loss of energy.

➤ Feeling restless and hyperactive, or being very passive and withdrawn.

➤ Lots of aches and pains, especially nausea, diarrhea or constipation, headaches, and back pain.

➤ Falling grades, skipping school.

➤ Trouble getting along with family and friends.

➤ Rebellion, brushes with the law, doing dangerous things.

➤ Using alcohol or drugs to dull pain.

➤ Thoughts of suicide.[6]

These are patterns that can suggest depression. Mental-health professionals, however, use a shorter list of symptoms to diagnose depression: mood disturbance, not enjoying life, change in eating patterns, change in sleeping patterns, not being able to think clearly, change in concentration, change in physical activity, loss of energy, and thinking about, or actually trying, suicide.[7] A person suffering from major depression must have five or more of these symptoms for at least two weeks, and the symptoms

*D*epression can affect anyone, regardless of how perfect they seem. Washington State University basketball player Steve Slotemaker announced in February 1999 that he had been suffering from clinical depression for six years. Slotemaker did not play his freshman year because of depression.

must make daily life difficult.[8] A major depression can be broken down even further into mild, moderate, or severe depression.[9]

Who Suffers From Depression?

The exact number of people suffering from depression is not really known because so many people do not know they have it and never get help. Mental-health professionals think that 10 to 15 percent of women and 5 to 12 percent of men—that is, 10 to 20 million Americans—suffer from depression.[10]

Rates of depression are going up. No one knows why, or if it is just that depression is being diagnosed more often. If you divide the people in our country into two age groups—over forty and under forty—those in the younger group are three times more likely to be depressed than those over forty. Even very young children can be depressed.[11] Eighty percent of people with depression never realize it, or at least never get help for it.[12]

As for rates of teen depression, the National Institute of Mental Health says that 1.5 million people under the age of eighteen, three girls for every guy, suffer from depression.[13] During any one year, 8 to 9 percent of children between the ages of ten and thirteen suffer a major depression, and it usually lasts for about a year.[14] Rates go up at puberty. The rate is higher for girls as they get older; 16 percent of girls between the ages of fourteen and sixteen are depressed.[15]

What Causes Depression?

Major depression often comes after something bad happens in a person's life, such as the death of a loved one or divorce. Studies show that those kinds of events are most important in a first time depression and less important in depression that comes back.[16]

How did Kelly know that her depression was not just a short "blue" time but something more serious? "Real depression is different because it's every day," she says,

> You hurt so much, you can't stop the crying. It goes on for a long time. You don't have good days and bad days—they're all bad days. Nothing is ever different, you are always sad, you always think, "Why does this have to happen to me, why is my life so terrible, why do I have it so bad?" You can't concentrate on anything. You don't go out with your friends, you don't have any fun. You don't want to get out of bed, you just want to sleep. Your friends stop calling because you don't call back. You don't have any answers.[17]

Dr. Longeway offers a few more things to think about:

> Usually, if you can see something in your life that would be upsetting to anyone and it makes you feel bad for a short time, that's a normal reaction. Chronic and major depression are really biological, genetic-related diseases; they are very different from a sad feeling when something goes wrong. But a very stressful life event that you aren't able to get over on your own can set you up for depression if you don't get help with it.[18]

Disorders Associated With Depression

Although dysthymic disorder and major depression are the two main types of depressive disorders, there are other types of disorders that are associated with depression. These other disorders are important to mention because a person who is feeling blue, without being clinically depressed, may actually be showing symptoms of one of these ailments.

Bipolar disorder. We all have mood swings from happy to sad, but people with manic depression, now often called bipolar disorder, have extreme mood swings. The swings do not always have anything to do with what is happening in the person's life. The shifts from mood to mood often come in cycles: The person will be jumpy, too active and "high," then will fall into a deep depression. Most people are normal between the cycles, but 20 to 30 percent have problems even between periods of being high or depressed.[19]

About 3 percent of Americans have bipolar disorder. Although the condition is less common than major depression, bipolar people are more likely to commit suicide than depressed people. In fact, 10 to 15 percent of the people who suffer from bipolar disorder take their own lives. That is more than any other mental disorder.[20]

Like depression, bipolar disorder runs in families. People who have it have high rates of child abuse, violent behavior, divorce, or antisocial behavior. Kids with it often skip school and get failing grades.

A milder form of bipolar disorder is called cyclothymic disorder. Like dysthymic disorder, it is a chronic condition. This means that the mood swings in cyclothymic disorder are not as extreme as those in bipolar disorder, but go on for a longer period of time (at least two years).[21]

Seasonal affective disorder (SAD). Some people

become very sleepy and depressed in the winter because of the loss of light. Because the depression only happens in the winter, it is called seasonal affective disorder (SAD). The degree of depression can range from mild to severe. The symptoms can include a change in appetite, weight gain, a drop in energy, oversleeping, a hard time concentrating, being irritable, and a craving for carbohydrates. These symptoms occur only in the fall and winter and go away in the spring.

Although about 10 million Americans have SAD, many people do not realize that they have it or that

Joann Prosser uses a full-spectrum light box to lessen the effects of SAD. Doctors estimate that 10 percent of the people in the rainy section of Oregon where Prosser lives may also suffer from this disorder.

it can be treated. Doctors think that SAD happens because the body cannot control serotonin and melatonin levels in winter's low light. Serotonin and melatonin are brain chemicals that affect a person's mood. SAD can be treated by sitting in front of a certain type of very strong light from half an hour to several hours a day. Regular light bulbs will not work. Therapy lights are ten to twenty times brighter than regular room light.

Adjustment disorder with depressed mood. This disorder is what happens when one of those bad things occurs, such as divorce or death of a parent, loss of a friend, or not making the team. Mental-health professionals look for a loss (parent, friend, pet, activity, home) or a big life change (parents getting divorced, moving to a new town). Most kids can think of some other things that might set off a depressed mood for them. If it goes on for more than a couple of weeks, the person may need to talk to someone about his or her feelings to help get back to normal.

Chapter 3

What Causes Depression?

What causes someone to catch a cold? A person who has a cold sneezing in his face? Not getting enough sleep for a few nights? Never eating any fruits or vegetables? Those things could all be part of the reason why sometimes a person can fight off a cold and sometimes he or she cannot.

In some ways it is the same with depression. The exact cause is not known, but there are several factors that are part of why most times people stay happy and mentally healthy, but some people have feelings of sadness that turn into a major depression.

Mental-health professionals who study depression say there are several types of causes. We will divide them into three categories: genetic influences, biochemical factors, and life stresses.

Genetic Influences

Do people inherit depression from their parents in the same way they inherit brown eyes? It is not quite that simple. Yet, depression does run in families, as it did in Annie's family. "There is a strong genetic pattern for severe forms of depression," says Dr. Longeway. "If you have other people in your family who have been depressed, it puts you at higher risk."[1]

Statistics show that depression is one and a half to three times more common in children or brothers or sisters of someone who has it.[2] Other studies have looked at relatives of people who are depressed and also found higher rates of depression in them.[3] The risk is especially high if it is a parent who is depressed. If one parent is depressed, the child has a 25 percent chance of also being depressed. If both parents are depressed, the risk for the children gets as high as 75 percent.[4] Some studies have looked at twins and found that if one identical twin has depression, the other has a 60 to 70 percent chance of being depressed also, even if the two were raised apart. The risk is only 25 percent if the twins are fraternal (not identical), or for non-twin brothers and sisters.[5]

Does that mean that if a parent or some other relative is depressed, someone is doomed to be depressed also? No. Depression is not like eye or hair color, which are directly inherited. But the tendency may be, especially if someone has a really big life stress, that genetic influences could cause depression.

Biochemical Factors

Knowing a little about how the brain works helps to understand the role brain chemistry plays in depression. Nerve cells cluster in "control centers" in the brain. Fibers, called axons, which look like fine hairs, sprout from those centers. Nerve cells talk to

How People in History Saw Depression

✓ A Greek doctor, Hippocrates, in the fifth century B.C., thought depression was caused by what he called the four humors of the body—blood, yellow bile, black bile, and phlegm—getting out of balance, especially when there was too much black bile.

✓ Aristotle, a hundred years later, thought depression was caused by a person's bile getting too cold. Treatment was letting out some blood, applying massage, telling the patient stories, and playing games.

✓ During the Middle Ages, doctors knew there was a link between depression and suicide. They treated depression with bathing and having the patient talk to family and friends.

✓ Eighteenth-century doctors dropped the idea of bile as causing depression, and said it came from blood, lymph, and animal spirits not moving around the body correctly.

✓ Nineteenth-century doctors knew that depression could be hereditary. One German psychiatrist suggested treating patients with the highly addictive drug opium.

Source: Dianne Hales, *The Encyclopedia of Health: Depression* (New York: Chelsea House Publishers, 1989) pp. 26-35.

one another by sending electrical signals through the axons. When an electrical signal reaches the end of an axon it needs a "bridge" to take it across the gap to the next axon. Those bridges are chemicals called neurotransmitters. Depression, as well other mental illnesses, can be caused when these chemical messengers get out of whack. Two transmitters especially, norepinephrine and serotonin, seem to be important in depression.[6] Some drugs for treating depression work by changing these brain chemicals. Brain chemistry may be a big part of the reason for the depression in Annie's family, and may be why the medicine she is taking is starting to help.

Life Stresses

Life can bring some big blows. Kids who have lots of support from parents and friends can usually handle them without becoming depressed. But some people do not have those support systems, and some have the genetic pattern or the out-of-balance brain chemicals that put them at risk. Drop a big stress into their life and they sink. "It's as if the stress is the trigger to a biological disorder, the depression," explains Dr. Longeway.[7]

What are some of those stresses? Stress is different for each person, but here are some common ones.

Family breakup. Parents getting divorced is one of the biggest stresses teenagers face. Judith Wallerstein, a psychologist, followed kids for ten years after their parents divorced. In her study, "California Children of Divorce," she found that more than a third of the children were depressed five years after the split-up, and many were still troubled ten years later.[8] Divorce can set off a chain of other changes: less attention from parents as they deal with their own problems, moving, having a lower income, learning to live with a new parent, and new brothers and sisters if one or both parents gets married again.

Having parents who just "aren't there." Cold parents who are not very interested in their kids, or who let them raise themselves, may be setting their kids up for depression.

A parent who is an alcoholic or uses drugs. Kids whose parents are lost in a world of drinking or drug use often find they have to take care of themselves, perhaps even younger brothers and sisters. Hiding the parent's drug or alcohol use can also be stressful.

Parents whose standards are too high. Most parents want their kids to do well, but a few have such high standards that no one could possibly meet them. Kids who feel like they can never do anything right can be under a lot of stress, especially if they think their parents' love depends on doing well.

Family illness. If a parent, brother, sister, or grandparent gets very sick, the whole family's life may revolve around that person. Kids in the family can feel forgotten while trying to cope with their own grief, and may feel guilty for being jealous of the attention the sick person gets.

Not having friends. Feeling different, awkward, left out, or rejected can set kids up for depression. Teens who think they may be lesbian or gay can be at high risk. So are kids who develop sexually either very early or very late—being different from every-one else can cause a problem.

Not doing well at school. Some kids are just better at schoolwork than others. Some students find school a struggle, especially if they have learning disabilities or attention deficit disorder. School problems can be a symptom of depression, but they can also help to cause it.

Losing someone or something important. When kids lose someone or something very dear it can be very hard. It can be a parent, grandparent, brother, sister, friend, boyfriend or girlfriend, pet—it does not matter. If it was important and loved, losing it can mean real grief. Trying to just not think about any of these losses can set a teen up for depression.

Getting sick or hurt. A few young people get a disease or are hurt in an accident. Those things can change a person's whole life. Looking very different, or adjusting to being disabled can set off a depression.

How Common Is Depression?

✓In any one year, 8 to 9 percent of children age ten to thirteen have a major depression. Rates go up as kids get older; they are higher for teens. The rate is as high as 16 percent in teenage girls.

✓Dysthymia (long-term, lower-level depression) is only half as common as major depression, but it lasts much longer.

✓People who have dysthymia are more likely to have major depression later.

Source: Barbara Ingersoll, Ph.D., and Sam Goldstein, Ph.D., Lonely, Sad and Angry: A Parent's Guide to Depression in Children and Adolescents (New York: Doubleday, 1995), p. 22.

Physical, emotional, or sexual abuse. Teens who are abused in any way, especially those who are raped, have an extremely high risk of depression. The worst thing a victim can do is to not tell anyone, because grief and anger can turn into depression. Most teens who go through some type of abuse need help to deal with it.

Drug and alcohol use. Drugs and alcohol depress the central nervous system. They affect brain chemistry. If a person has any tendency to depression, using drugs or alcohol will probably make it worse.[9]

Why is it that some teens have stresses in their lives and do just fine, while others are sucked down by depression? No one knows the answer to that question, but genetic influences and biochemical factors both play a part. Teens who have them do not always become depressed. People have a lot of control over what happens to them. They can make good decisions about getting help.

Chapter 4

Suicide: When Depression Turns Deadly

I really, seriously considered suicide," says Kelly. "I think about ninety-nine percent of my friends have thought about it. I have some friends who have actually tried it."[1]

Suicide Rates

The number of teens who commit suicide is much higher than many people realize. According to Catholic Charities, suicide is the third leading cause of death among people between the ages of fifteen and twenty-four. Nearly five thousand teens commit suicide each year, with thirty to fifty unsuccessful attempts for every one completed. Four times as many guys kill themselves as girls, but girls try twice as often (guys may kill themselves more often because they are more likely to use guns, whereas more girls use drug overdoses and are rescued before the pills take effect). At least half the teens who commit suicide have a drug or alcohol abuse problem.[2]

The rate for suicide has stayed the same, or even gone up, for many years. The rate is going up fastest among young men age fifteen to twenty-four (tripled since 1950), among young African-American men in the same age group (up 66 percent in the last fifteen years), and among young women in the same age group (doubled since 1950).[3]

The age of suicides is dropping also. The rate for children age ten to fourteen has doubled in the past fifteen years, according to the American Federation for Suicide Prevention.[4]

Despite all the publicity about suicide, Americans still do not understand it very well. The American Federation for Suicide Prevention found that fewer than half of all Americans surveyed thought depression was a health problem; two of every five said depression and suicide were signs of being a weak person.[5]

Myths About Suicide

People believe a lot of myths about suicide. These myths are not true, and belief in them can sometimes unintentionally lead to disastrous situations. It is important to know the truth behind these myths so that one may react appropriately when certain situations arise. Some of these myths include

> ➢ *People who talk about suicide do not do it.* We are not just talking about the teen who says, "I'll just die if I don't get a part in the play." We are talking about serious statements such as "I wish I weren't here anymore," or "You'll be sorry when I'm gone." Teens who talk about suicide do kill themselves.

> ➢ *If people would just look at the bright side, they would feel better.* That is part of the view

*S*uicide is the third leading cause of death for young adults. Young males are four times more likely than females to kill themselves.

that depression and feeling suicidal mean you are not a strong person. "You're just not trying hard enough to pull out of it," someone might say. But depression, which often leads to suicide, is an illness, not a weakness.

➤ *Talking about suicide, or trying it, are just ways to get attention.* No, they are signs of serious problems. Everybody enjoys attention; that is normal. But attempting suicide or even talking about it is not normal.

➤ *If the person seems to cheer up, the crisis is over.* It may mean the person has decided to commit suicide. If the person is happily giving away all his or her favorite things, that may be another bad sign.

➤ *People who commit suicide are mentally ill.* Many are, but some are not. Certainly, most are depressed. Many feel hopeless. "Not everyone who is depressed is suicidal, but most people who are suicidal are depressed," says Debra Reid, a certified clinical social worker who has worked a great deal with depressed teenagers. "Many times kids who try suicide do not want to die, they want to stop the pain. They want to be taken seriously."[6] Up to 15 percent of depressed people die from suicide.[7]

What puts a teenager at risk of suicide? As with depression, both biological and life stress factors play a part.

Biological Factors

Is there a gene for suicide? No, but research shows that there are some biological and genetic factors involved in causing a person to commit suicide. By studying the brains of suicide victims, researchers have found that most of them have low levels of the neurotransmitter serotonin. It seems to even out moods and keep a brake on the impulse to do reckless things. The director of the Mental Health Clinical Research Center for the Study of Suicidal Behavior said that people who are low in serotonin are more likely to be aggressive, and may have trouble controlling the impulse to kill themselves.[8]

It also seems that suicide runs in families. The author Ernest Hemingway killed himself; so did his father, brother, sister, and granddaughter, the actress Margaux Hemingway.[9] It may be from inherited, abnormal brain chemicals; or it could be that the taboo [moral restriction] against suicide becomes weaker when someone else in the family does it.

Life Stress Factors

There are a whole group of life events that can raise the risk of suicide.

The same losses that cause depression—parents' divorcing, death of a close family member or friend, breakup of a romance—can have an effect. Having parents who have their own problems with depression or alcoholism, or who are cold or unloving, can also be a factor.

Feeling alone and having few friends can put someone at risk. Some teens do not seem to know how to make friends and get along with others. Or friendly teens may withdraw when they are depressed. In either case, the lack of a warm, caring support group can raise risk.

Being a victim of abuse such as rape can be a

Facts About Suicide

✓ Suicide is the third leading cause of death for teenagers in the United States.

✓ The rate of suicide for teens has tripled in the last twenty years.

✓ Most suicides happen in the person's house, between 3:00 P.M. and midnight.

✓ Nearly five thousand teenagers commit suicide every year. There are about thirty to fifty attempts for every one that succeeds.

✓ Girls try suicide more often, but boys succeed more often. In the most recent year that statistics were available, there were 21.7 suicides for every 100,000 males between fifteen and twenty-four, but only 4.4 for every 100,000 females in the same age group.

✓ The reason more boys succeed is because they often use violent means, such as guns or hanging. Girls most often use pills, and can be saved from an overdose if found early enough.

✓ Half of teens who commit suicide abuse drugs or alcohol.

✓ Almost all teens who commit suicide have at least one mental or substance-abuse disorder. Over half have more than one.

✓ Teens who have friends or classmates who have committed suicide may be at higher risk. Experts call these "cluster suicides."

Sources: *American Medical Association Family Medical Guide*, 3rd ed. (New York: Random House, 1994), p. 763; Catholic Charities, "Help to Prevent Teen Suicide," n.d., <www.advinc.com/-tmd/suicide.html> (October 5, 1998).

huge factor. Lesbian, gay, or bisexual teens (who may feel rejected by society) try suicide two or three times more often than heterosexual teens do.[10]

Aggression and rebellion are a bad sign. Not all teens who drive recklessly, fool around with guns, drive drunk, or have run-ins with the law are depressed or suicidal. But some are. "Suicide is sometimes seen as the greatest expression of anger," says Reid.[11] Drug and alcohol abuse can be a factor, too. Drugs and alcohol can cloud a person's thinking and make it harder to control actions. A person who is depressed may be more likely to try suicide if he or she is drunk.

Suicide of other teens or teen idols can influence some kids. When a young person commits suicide, often several others in the same town—or even far away if the suicide gets national attention—will do the same thing. Suicide rates can go up 10 percent in the weeks following a suicide reported in the press. Mental-health professionals call this a "suicide cluster."[12] Teens who admire a person such as rock star Kurt Cobain or writer Sylvia Plath, who both committed suicide, may be at extra risk.

What should a person who is feeling really down and thinking about suicide do? "Talk about it," says Debra Reid. "If you are really at the end of your rope and thinking about suicide, talk to someone. Talk to your parents if you can, but don't expect that your parents will be able to fix everything for you. You may need to talk to a counselor."[13]

Annie says, "Don't blame yourself for this; it's not your fault. Even though it's hard, talk to your family and friends because they are the ones who will be there for you. If you push them away, you won't have that support."[14]

*S*ome people do not win the fight against depression. Although Kurt Cobain (second from right) enjoyed financial and artistic success with the band Nirvana, he committed suicide in 1994.

Suicidal feelings are not something someone can deal with alone. Help is there, but do not wait too long. Remember that feeling depressed is the greatest risk for suicide—the National Alliance for the Mentally Ill says that as many as 75 percent of suicides are caused by depression.[15] So do not put off getting help.

"Time is valuable when you are dealing with depression and suicidal thoughts," says Reid. "Give yourself enough time to deal with it, to see that life can work out and you can be happy again."[16]

Chapter 5

How Do I Get Over This Thing?

Depression is not a sentence to a lifetime of feeling blue," says Dr. Longeway. "It can be helped by therapy and medicine. Taking pills alone won't cure a depression, but medicine can allow a person to have enough energy to find new solutions to problems and new ways to cope with stress."[1] What should someone do if he or she is feeling depressed and it is not going away?

Self-Help for Depression

When feeling down, people can do a lot of things that can help lift their mood. These activities can not only stop someone from feeling blue, but are also good guidelines for leading a healthy, happy life in general.

Exercise. Walking, running, or biking can all help to lift a mood. In fact, any physical activity, whether it be recreational sports, lifting weights, or yoga can help raise a person's spirits. Exercise helps with sleep, perks up appetite, and can release brain chemicals that help a person feel better.

Do fun things. Spending time with friends rather

than sitting home brooding can help. One of the things Kelly did was to make herself be with other people instead of withdrawing. "When I'm out with my friends, I get to laugh and be happy and not think about all the bad things that are going on in my life," she says.[2]

Follow normal daily routines. Staying in bed all day can make a person feel even more depressed. Getting up, taking a shower, getting dressed, and eating the proper meals, however, can make a person feel better.

Avoid alcohol and drugs. Substance abuse makes depression even worse. Even stimulant drugs, which are supposed give people a boost, make a person feel even worse than before once they wear off.

If these self-help things do not help, then the person may have dysthymic disorder or major depression. He or she will probably need professional help. Many teens start by talking to their parents. If that is not possible, then the person should talk to another trusted adult, such as a grandparent, teacher, school guidance counselor, minister, rabbi, priest, or family doctor. Many of them will know where to find help.

Professional Help for Depression

There are several different types of therapy. Depending on the person, most patients respond better to a certain type of therapy than others do. Sometimes, a patient benefits from an eclectic type of therapy, meaning that two or more types of therapies are combined.

Cognitive therapy. This helps people change the

*B*ecause of the shorter days and gray skies, some people suffer from seasonal affective disorder during the winter months.

way they think about things. People work on bad thinking patterns and learn to think in more realistic ways.

Behavioral therapy. The mental-health professional uses rewards to change the patient's harmful behavior to healthier ways of behaving.

Interpersonal or family therapy. This type of therapy helps people improve communication skills and build better relationships with family and friends.

Insight therapy. The doctor helps a person understand conflicts hidden in the unconscious mind. This method is used less often with teens because it means spending a long time reflecting back on the person's childhood.[3]

What to expect in therapy. Most of all, says Dr. Longeway, a counselor or therapist provides a safe place where a teen can face whatever is upsetting him or her, and find ways to solve problems. "A therapist can help you use your strengths, your supports, your resources to fight the depression," she says. "He or she may help you think of ways to cope that you couldn't think of yourself."[4]

The first step in therapy, says Kathleen Neville, a clinical social worker who works with teens, is to develop a trusting relationship between the client and the therapist. "I try to break the ice," she says. "I may ask, 'Where do you go to school? Do you like your teachers? Do you have a lot of friends? What do you like to do best in your spare time? What kind of movies do you like?' I try to get to know the person."[5]

Once that is done, she says, the therapist will move into the area that is causing trouble. "I might start by saying, 'I know you are having some struggles.' I don't ask first thing if the person is depressed, but by the end of the session I will start to talk about it."[6] One of the things a therapist initially does, Neville says, is what counselors call "validating" the person's feelings. That means saying the client is not wrong to feel the way he or she does. "In Kelly's case I would talk about how hard it is to be in the middle of a divorce and go back and forth between two houses," she says.[7] That lets the client know the therapist understands, and that the issues are real.

"Next, I'll want to find out if the person has other adults to turn to: grandparents, aunts, uncles, perhaps a teacher," she says. "I'll also ask about friends."[8] Sometimes kids do not realize how much help and support they can get from the people around them.

The therapist will probably also work on finding out how the client thinks. Are his or her thoughts true? Kelly's were not when she thought her parents' divorce was her fault. "If what the person is thinking isn't true, we'll try to work on correcting the faulty thinking," Neville says.[9]

The therapist will have to ask some personal questions to understand what is going on inside, Neville says, such as about dreams or what the person is afraid of. He or she may ask if any of the person's friends or family members are also depressed. Another question is how physically active the person is, because many depressed people spend too much time lying around or sleeping. Eating patterns, especially if they have changed, might also come up. "I need to get the person to color in the blank screen about who he or she is," she says.[10]

A Depression Checklist

Photocopy this page. (Do not write in this book.)
Check the items that apply to you on the photocopy.

_____ I feel sad most of the time, and it never seems to lift.

_____ I feel guilty when bad things happen to other people, even if it is really not my fault.

_____ I have lost all interest in sports, music, my friends, and school.

_____ I just want to be left alone.

_____ I am tired all the time; I want to sleep during the day.

_____ I have trouble sleeping at night.

_____ I have either gained or lost a lot of weight recently.

_____ I feel restless most of the time. I cannot sit still or relax.

_____ I have trouble concentrating.

_____ I think I am ugly, dumb, and worthless a lot of the time.

_____ My friends ask me what is wrong, or tell me I seem sad.

_____ I think about death a lot. I admire celebrities who have killed themselves.

_____ I like to do dangerous things, like driving recklessly or fooling around with weapons.

_____ Sometimes I hurt myself just a little bit because it makes me feel better.

_____ I really wish I could just stop living.

If you only checked one or two items, you are probably not depressed (unless one of the things you checked was the last one). If you checked more than two, you may need to talk to someone about dealing with your down mood. If you checked most or all of them, show this list to a trusted adult—you probably need help. If you checked the last two, you need to get help right away.

Sources: Barbara Ingersoll, Ph.D., and Sam Goldstein, Ph.D., *Lonely, Sad and Angry: A Parent's Guide to Depression in Children and Adolescents* (New York: Doubleday, 1995); Kathleen McCoy, Ph.D., *Understanding Your Teenager's Depression* (New York: Perigee Books, 1994); Essie Lee and Richard Wortmann, M.D., *Down Is Not Out: Teenagers and Depression* (New York: Julian Messner, 1986); Telephone interview with Kathleen Longeway, Ph.D., August 6, 1998; Telephone interview with Kathleen Neville, CICSW, March 11, 1999.

The therapist will ask if the person is having any suicidal thoughts. If the answer is yes, he or she may need to go into a hospital to stay safe until the crisis is past.

Sometimes during therapy very personal information comes out, such as sexual activity. A therapist, Neville says, may encourage the person to talk about it because it might be part of what is causing the depression. Sometimes teens worry that the therapist will tell their parents they have been sexually active. "That I won't do," Neville says. "I may tell the person, 'This is not safe physically and emotionally, and I think you need to talk to your parents about it,' but I wouldn't tell the parents."[11]

A therapist may refer the person to a psychiatrist—a medical doctor with special training in mental illness—to see if medicine is needed.

Medications

Certain types of depressions are caused by body chemicals not working right, so it makes sense that getting the chemicals in better balance can help. That is done with medicines called antidepressants.

Dr. Gregory Schmidt, a psychiatrist who works with teenagers, says, "Antidepressants are used more today than in the past because they are very effective now. Probably seventy or eighty percent of people with depression will respond well to an antidepressant."[12]

Dr. Schmidt explains that antidepressants work on brain cells.

There are receptors on the cells that respond to the neurotransmitters made by other cells. Sometimes, in depression, the receptor's response gets out of normal range. The

*C*omedian Drew Carey suffered from depression as a young adult. Carey was able to take control of his life and now has a successful television career.

medication works on the receptors to make them either more or less sensitive. You can think of it as tuning a radio, getting the receptors back into normal range.[13]

There are many different kinds of anti-depressants. Tricyclic antidepressants have been used for many years. Some of them are Elavil, Norpramin, Tofranil, and Pamelor. They may have side effects such as dry mouth, blurred vision, constipation, or sleepiness. Newer antidepressants called selective serotonin uptake inhibitors (SSRIs) can help without the side effects. Some of them are Prozac, Paxil, and Zoloft. "There have been some recent studies with teens showing there is good benefit from these new drugs," says Dr. Schmidt. "And drug companies are developing more all the time."[14]

But, do they work? Dr. Schmidt says they do. "They help, but it's always important to keep the focus on what's going on in someone's life and helping them learn to deal with it better."[15]

In other words, there are no magic pills that will take depression away by themselves. While they can be very helpful, most people, like Annie, still need to do the work of understanding why they are depressed and finding solutions to their problems. That work can be easier to do, though, when medicine breaks up the clouds of gloom.

Sometimes teens resist the idea of taking antidepressants because they worry about taking a drug. Dr. Schmidt has some answers to common questions.

> ➤ Are antidepressants addictive? Antidepressants do not make a person feel high, so there is no danger of addiction. "If somebody who isn't depressed takes Prozac he would not feel any better, or feel high," he says. "The drugs only make your mood normal; they don't create anything artificial."[16]

> ➤ What about side effects? All drugs have some side effects. The newer antidepressants do not have nearly as many as the older ones did. "The most common side effect is feeling a little hyper, not sleeping as well," says Dr. Schmidt. "Sometimes there is

some stomach upset. But the side effects only happen to a small number of people."[17]

➢ Is mixing antidepressants with other drugs or alcohol dangerous? "Mixing any drug with street drugs or alcohol is dangerous," Dr. Schmidt says. Some antidepressants can affect the way the liver breaks down other drugs, which makes any other drug stronger. Alcohol makes a person more depressed, so it many work against an anti-depressant, he says.[18]

Hospitalization

There are some times when a person suffering from depression needs to check into a hospital, especially if he or she is suicidal. "Hospitalization is a much shorter process than it used to be," Dr. Schmidt says. "It's used only when the risk of self-harm is too high for safe treatment to happen outside."[19]

In the hospital a person will spend a lot of time talking to mental-health professionals and with groups of other patients. Patients wear their own clothes, and the rooms look more like a dormitory than they do the images of hospital rooms from television and the movies. Teens are sometimes frightened of going to the hospital, but for someone with serious depression, it can be a safe place to get better.

Getting better—that is the important thing. "Depression is very treatable," says Dr. Longeway. "It's not something to be ashamed of or to feel guilty about. It's like any other physical illness. Most people get through it and do well."[20]

Chapter 6

When a Friend Is Depressed

How common is depression among teenagers? If Kelly's friends are typical, it is very common. Although she may be exaggerating, she did say that she thinks "ninety-nine percent" of her friends have considered suicide, and she knows a couple who have actually tried it.[1]

Friends can be a depressed person's first source of help, a lifeline that saves them. That is a big responsibility if you are the friend of someone who is depressed.

How can a person know if a friend is just having a blue time or is seriously depressed? By looking at the symptoms of depression and seeing how many of them apply to the friend. If there are more than a couple symptoms, and if they hang on for more than two weeks, the friend may be depressed.

Sometimes the person who is depressed may not know it. Depression can affect a person's mind so much, he or she cannot think clearly. The person may feel helpless, and think there is no hope or help anywhere. A friend may be the only voice saying, "There is hope, this awful feeling can go away."

Anytime a teenager thinks a friend is suffering

from depression, it is important that he or she does not try to aid the friend alone. This is not something a teen can handle without help. Go to a trusted adult right away. The friend may be angry at first, but that is better than having a friend who is dead. If the friend's parents care, they may be the best place to start. If that is not possible, the person should talk to his or her own parents, a trusted teacher, school psychologist or guidance counselor, doctor or nurse, minister, rabbi, or priest.

What Not to Do

There are some things someone whose friend is depressed should never do. Doing these things can actually make the friend worse off than he or she was before.

Do not promise to keep things secret. If a friend says she is depressed or thinking about suicide, secrecy is not a promise to keep. No one likes to tell a friend's secret, but having a dead friend is even worse.

Do not believe the myths that people who talk about suicide do not do it. Take anything a friend says, such as "I wish I were dead" or "You'd be better off without me," seriously. Also take it seriously if a friend wants to give away his or her favorite things—that may mean the person is planning suicide. Do not think that just because a depressed person is suddenly more cheerful that the crisis is over. The friend may have decided to commit suicide and made a plan; that can make the person seem more happy.

Do not judge the person. Do not say something like, "How can you even think about doing such an awful thing?" Making the person feel ashamed or guilty will not help. It could push him or her into doing

Smoking and Depression: A Link?

Investigators from the University of California, San Diego, and San Diego State University did a study of 6,863 teens age twelve to eighteen. It showed

✓ Teen smokers were twice as likely to develop symptoms of depression. Also, depressed teenagers were more likely to start smoking than nondepressed teens.

✓ Female smokers ran a higher risk: 15.3 percent were depressed, compared with 8.1 percent of male smokers.

✓ The study did not examine why there is a link between depression and smoking.

Source: Philip W. Long, M.D., "Young Smokers More Likely to Suffer Depression." *The Medical Post*, April 9, 1996, <http://www.mentalhealth.com/mag1/p5m-dp04.html> (October 5, 1998).

something dangerous. Do not ever dare a friend to do something by saying something like, "You wouldn't have the nerve to do anything." Even if it is done in a kidding way, the friend could take it seriously.[2]

Do not try to make a friend get well by yourself. A friend cannot do that. The depressed person needs professional help, and that is not something a friend can provide.

What to Do to Help a Friend

Besides the "do nots," there are also some things a friend should do when someone is depressed or suicidal. By taking these actions, one can help put a friend on the road to recovery. Even if all these actions are taken, however, a professional should still be consulted.

Tell a responsible adult. A teenager cannot handle this alone. Consult his or her parents, aunt or uncle, priest, rabbi, teacher, guidance counselor, or any other trusted adult. They can help the friend find professional help.

Be there for the friend. Listen. It can be very comforting for someone to hear how much a friend likes him or her, or how much people care. If the friend's talking about suicide is frightening, say so. Let the friend know how much he or she is valued and would be missed. Encourage the person to talk. Ask questions such as, "Have you thought about killing

*M*ike Wallace, host of *60 Minutes*, and Tipper Gore, wife of politician Al Gore, have both battled depression. Here, Tipper Gore and Wallace discuss depression at the White House Conference on Mental Health on June 7, 1999.

yourself?" That will not put ideas into his or her head that are not already there. If the person says yes, ask how he or she plans to do it. Then take that information to an adult.

Help the friend solve problems, but if they are too much for a teen to deal with, tell the person so. Suggest professional help. Offer to go with the friend to see an expert. Point out that problems are temporary; that there are solutions. Also tell her that suicide is a permanent way to deal with a temporary problem.

If the person seems to think all the time about the suicide of someone he or she knows or someone in the media, get the friend to talk about it. Suggest he or she get help. Tell an adult.

If you think the friend is going to try suicide, stay with him or her. Take away anything dangerous like knives, pills, or a gun. Get help. Call an adult or a suicide hot line (they are listed in the Yellow Pages in most cities under hot lines or help lines). If the person has already done something, do not wait. Call 911 or another emergency help number to get him or her to a hospital.[3]

If a Friend Commits Suicide

Sometimes a person still commits suicide, even though people try to stop it. It is very important for that person's friends to remember that it is not anyone's fault. It is shocking and tragic when a young person takes his or her life, but blaming does not help. Do not fall into the trap of thinking, "If only we had done more."[4] Sometimes friends of someone who has committed suicide need help to deal with it.

American Association of Suicidology
4201 Connecticut Ave., NW., Suite 408
Washington, DC 20008
(202) 237-2280
<http://www.suicidology.org./>

American Mental Health Foundation
2 East Eighty-sixth Street
New York, NY 10028
(212) 737-9027

Center for Mental Health Services:
Knowledge Exchange Network
P.O. Box 42490
Washington, DC 20015
(800) 789-2647
<http://www.mentalhealth.org>

Depression Awareness, Recognition and
Treatment Project
National Institute of Mental Health
DEPRESSION
6001 Executive Blvd., Rm. 8184,
MSC 9663
Bethesda, MD 20892-9663
(800) 421-4211
<http://www.nimh.nih.gov/depression/index.htm>

National Alliance for the Mentally Ill
200 North Glebe Road, Suite 1015
Arlington, VA 22203-3754
(800) 950-6264
<http://www.nami.org/>

National Depression Association
(312) 642-0049

National Depressive and Manic Depressive
Association
730 North Franklin Street, Suite 501
Chicago, IL 60610-3526
(800) 826-3632
<http://www.ndmda.org/>

National Institute of Mental Health
NIMH Public Inquiries
6001 Executive Blvd., Rm. 8184,
MSC 9663
Bethesda, MD 20892-9663
(301) 443-4513
<http://www.nimh.nih.gov>

National Mental Health Association
1021 Prince Street
Alexandria, VA 22314-2971
(800) 969-6642
<http://www.nmha.org>

Chapter 1. Two Stories of Depression

1. Personal interview with "Kelly," September 8, 1998.
2. Ibid.
3. Ibid.
4. Ibid.
5. Ibid.
6. Ibid.
7. Ibid.
8. Ibid.
9. Ibid.
10. Ibid.
11. Ibid.
12. Ibid.
13. Telephone interview with "Annie," March 27, 1999.
14. Ibid.
15. Ibid.
16. Ibid.
17. Ibid.
18. Ibid.
19. Ibid.
20. Ibid.
21. National Institute of Mental Health, quoted in Sabrina Solin, "Depression," *Seventeen*, April 1995, p. 155.
22. Barbara Ingersoll, Ph.D., and Sam Goldstein, Ph.D., *Lonely, Sad & Angry: A Parent's Guide to Depression in Children & Adolescents* (New York: Doubleday, 1995), p. 22.

Chapter 2. What Is This Thing Called Depression?

1. Laurence Urdang, ed., *Mosby's Medical and Nursing Dictionary* (St. Louis: C.V. Mosby Company, 1983), p. 316.

2. Telephone interview with Kathleen Longeway, Ph.D., August 6, 1998.

3. Ibid.

4. *Diagnostic and Statistical Manual of Mental Disorders*, 4th ed. (Washington, D.C.: American Psychiatric Association, 1994), p. 343.

5. Ibid., p. 347

6. Adapted from Kathleen McCoy, Ph.D., *Understanding Your Teenager's Depression* (New York: Perigee Books, 1994), pp. 76–83; Essie Lee and Richard Wortmann, M.D., *Down Is Not Out: Teenagers and Depression* (New York: Julian Messner, 1986), pp. 72–73; Centerpoint Institute for Human Development, P.C. "Depression: Learn to Manage the Lows in Life," n.d., <www.centerpointsa.com/depress.html> (October, 1998); Telephone interview with Kathleen Longeway, Ph.D., August 6, 1998.

7. *Diagnostic and Statistical Manual of Mental Disorders*, p. 327.

8. Ibid., p. 327.

9. Ibid. p. 339.

10. *Diagnostic and Statistical Manual of Mental Disorders*, p. 341; Shirley N. Gruen, Ph.D., *Shirley N. Gruen, Ph.D.: Clinical Psychologist* "Depression Truly Is a National Health Crisis," n.d., <http://talkingdoc.com/articles/depression-crisis.htm> (October 5, 1998).

11. Barbara Ingersoll, Ph.D., and Sam Goldstein, Ph.D., *Lonely, Sad & Angry: A Parent's Guide to Depression in Children & Adolescents* (New York: Doubleday, 1995), p. 23.

12. Dianne Hales, *The Encyclopedia of Health: Depression* (New York: Chelsea House Publishers, 1989), p. 15.

13. National Institute of Mental Health, quoted in Sabrina Solin, "Depression," *Seventeen*, April 1995, p. 155.

14. Ingersoll, and Goldstein, p. 22.

15. Ibid, p. 22.

16. *Diagnostic and Statistical Manual of Mental Disorders*, p. 342.

17. Personal interview with "Kelly," September 8, 1998.

18. Telephone interview with Longeway.

19. *Diagnostic and Statistical Manual of Mental Disorders*, p. 353.

20. Meg Kissinger, "Suicide Rates Vex Families, Medical Profession," *The Milwaukee Journal-Sentinel*, August 2, 1998.

21. *Diagnostic and Statistical Manual of Mental Disorders*, pp. 362–363.

Chapter 3. What Causes Depression?

1. Telephone interview with Kathleen Longeway, Ph.D., August 6, 1998.

2. *Diagnostic and Statistical Manual of Mental Disorders*, 4th ed. (Washington, D.C.: American Psychiatric Association, 1994), p. 342.

3. Dante Cicchetti and Sheree Toth, "The Development of Depression in Children and Adolescent," *American Psychologist*, February 1998, p. 232.

4. Barbara Ingersoll, Ph.D., and Sam Goldstein, Ph.D., *Lonely, Sad & Angry: A Parent's Guide to Depression in Children & Adolescents* (New York: Doubleday, 1995), p. 73.

5. Kathleen McCoy, Ph.D., *Understanding Your Teenager's Depression* (New York: Perigee Books, 1994), p. 38.

6. Ingersoll and Goldstein, p. 77.

7. Telephone interview with Longeway.

8. Judith Wallerstein and Sandra Blakeslee, *Second Chances: Men, Women & Children a Decade After Divorce* (New York: Ticknor & Fields, 1989), pp. xxi–xxvi.

9. List developed from author interviews with Kathleen Longeway, Ph.D., August 6, 1998, and Kathleen Neville, March 3,1999; Barbara Ingersoll, Ph.D., and Sam Goldstein, Ph.D., *Lonely, Sad & Angry: A Parent's Guide to Depression in Children & Adolescents* (New York: Doubleday, 1995); Kathleen McCoy, Ph.D., *Understanding Your Teenager's Depression* (New York: Perigee Books, 1994).

Chapter 4. Suicide: When Depression Turns Deadly

1. Personal interview with "Kelly," September 8, 1998.

2. Catholic Charities, "Help to Prevent Teen Suicide, n.d., <www.advic.com/~tmd/suicide.html> (October 5, 1998).

3. Meg Kissinger, "Suicide Rates Vex Families, Medical Profession," *The Milwaukee Journal-Sentinel*, August 2, 1998.

4. Ibid.

5. Ibid.

6. Telephone interview with Debra Reid, CICSW, July 12, 1998.

7. *Diagnostic and Statistical Manual of Mental Disorders*, 4th ed. (Washington, D.C.: American Psychiatric Association, 1994), p. 340.

8. J. John Mann Mental Health Clinical Research Center for the Study of Suicidal Behavior, quoted in Kissinger.

9. Ibid.

10. Barbara Ingersoll, Ph.D., and Sam Goldstein, Ph.D., *Lonely, Sad and Angry: A Parent's Guide to Depression in Children and Adolescents* (New York: Doubleday, 1995), p. 128.

11. Telephone interview with Reid.

12. Ingersoll and Goldstein, pp. 129–130.

13. Telephone interview with Reid.

14. Telephone interview with "Annie," March 27, 1999.

15. National Alliance for the Mentally Ill, "The NAMI-Wisconsin Family and Consumer Resource Guide," February 1996, p. 8.

16. Telephone interview with Reid.

Chapter 5. How Do I Get Over This Thing?

1. Telephone interview with Kathleen Longeway, Ph.D., August 6, 1998.

2. Personal interview with "Kelly," September 8, 1998.

3. Adapted from Barbara Ingersoll, Ph.D., and Sam Goldstein, Ph.D., *Lonely, Sad & Angry: A Parent's Guide to Depression in Children & Adolescents* (New York: Doubleday, 1995), p. 79.

4. Telephone interview with Longeway.

5. Telephone interview with Kathleen Neville, CICSW, March 11, 1999.

6. Ibid.

7. Ibid.

8. Ibid.

9. Ibid.

10. Ibid.

11. Ibid.

12. Telephone interview with Gregory Schmidt, M.D., September 1, 1998.

13. Ibid.

14. Ibid.

15. Ibid.
16. Ibid.
17. Ibid.
18. Ibid.
19. Ibid.
20. Telephone interview with Longeway.

Chapter 6. When a Friend Is Depressed

1. Personal interview with "Kelly," September 8, 1998.

2. Adapted from SA\VE (Suicide Awareness\Voice of Education) publication, "What to Do If a Friend Has Depression: A Guide for Students," 1998; Dianne Hales, *The Encyclopedia of Health: Depression* (New York: Chelsea House Publishers, 1989), pp. 71–72.

3. Ibid.

4. Adapted from SA\VE, 1998.

antidepressant—A medicine that corrects a chemical imbalance in the brain, which helps many depressed people feel better.

axons—Fibers on nerve cells through which the cells send electrical signals to each other.

bipolar disorder— A mood disorder in which the person swings between being in a very elevated mood and a deep depression. Also called manic depression.

cluster suicide—A series of suicides that are triggered by another suicide, usually that of a celebrity or a peer.

cognitive therapy—A form of treatment for depression that helps the person correct negative thoughts or beliefs, and ones that are not true.

control centers—Portions of the brain where nerve cells cluster.

depression—A mood in which the person feels sad, hopeless, has low self-worth, finds it hard to concentrate, and does not sleep or eat normally. It may be caused by an imbalance of chemicals in the brain.

dysthymic disorder—Long-term, lower-level sadness and anxiety.

genetic—Having to do with genes, which determine the traits a person inherits.

major depression—Depression that is bad enough to prevent a person from living normally.

mood disorder—A mental-health category that includes depression and bipolar disorder.

neurotransmitter—A chemical that allows nerve impulses to jump across spaces between neurons in the brain.

psychotherapy—Treating a mental or emotional problem by talking to a trained mental-health professional.

seasonal affective disorder (SAD)—A condition in which a person becomes depressed due to the low light during the fall and winter months.

serotonin—A brain chemical that plays an important part in whether or not a person will become depressed.

Ayer, Eleanor. *Everything You Need to Know About . . . Depression*. New York: Rosen Publishing Group, 1997.

Carter, Sharon, and Clayton Lawrence, Ph.D. *Coping With Depression*. Center City, Minn.: Hazelden, 1997.

Cobain, Bev. *When Nothing Matters Anymore: A Survival Guide for Depressed Teens*. Minneapolis: Free Spirit Publishing, 1998.

Garland, Jane. *Depression Is the Pits, but I'm Getting Better: A Guide for Adolescents*. Washington, D.C.: Magination Press, 1997.

Hamburger, Lew, Ph.D. *Winning!: How Teens (And Other Humans) Can Beat Anger and Depression: A Handbook for Teens, Teachers, Parents, Therapists, and Counselors*. New York: Vantage Press, 1997.

Klebanoff, Susan, and Ellen Luborsky. *Ups and Downs: How to Beat the Blues and Teen Depression*. Los Angeles: Price, Stern, Sloan Publishing, 1998.

McCoy, Kathy. *Life Happens: A Teenager's Guide to Friends, Failure, Sexuality, Love, Rejection, Addiction, Peer Pressure, Families, Loss, Depression, Change*. New York: Perigee, 1996.

Meier, Paul. *Happiness Is a Choice for Teens*. Nashville: Nelson, Thomas, Inc., 1997

Schleifer, Jay. *Everything You Need to Know About Teen Suicide*. New York: Rosen Publishing Group, 1997.

Smith, Judie. *Drugs and Suicide*. New York: Rosen Publishing Group, 1995.

Stewart, Gail. *Teens & Depression*. San Diego: Lucent Books, 1998.

Weaver, Robyn M. *Depression*. San Diego: Lucent Books, 1998.

Weeldreyer, Laura. *Body Blues: Weight and Depression*. New York: Rosen Publishing Group, 1998.

Wolff, Lisa. *Teen Depression*. San Diego: Lucent Books, 1998.

Woog, Adam. *Suicide*. San Diego: Lucent Books, 1998.